WINE: A NO-SNOB GUIDE

Wine

A NO-SNOB GUIDE

Drink Outside the Box

LORI STEVENS

**ROCKRIDGE
PRESS**

For general information on our other products and services or to obtain technical support, please contact our Customer Care Department within the U.S. at (866) 744-2665, or outside the U.S. at (510) 253-0500.

Rockridge Press publishes its books in a variety of electronic and print formats. Some content that appears in print may not be available in electronic books, and vice versa.

Photography © by Stockfood/Westermann, Jan-Peter, p.2; Stocksy/Danil Nevsky, p.6; Stockfood/Plueckhahn, Clare, p.10; Stocksy/ Thomas Pickard, p.26; Stockfood/Sam Stowell, p.40; Stocksy/Andy Campbell, p.54; Stockfood/ Jennifer Martine, p.66; Stocksy/Sandra Cunningham, p.76; Stockfood/PhotoCuisine/ Hubert Taillard, p.88

ISBN: Print 978-1-62315-657-2
eBook 978-1-62315-658-9

CONTENTS

INTRODUCTION

*Y*ou march to the bar announcing your order: "Gin martini, extra dry, extra olives." Why gin over vodka?

At a backyard barbecue you head straight for the cooler, past the keg of craft beer. You ignore the Bud and grab an icy Corona. Why a Mexican lager over a pilsner or a kegged IPA? Why gin or Corona? Easy—you've tasted these before and learned what you enjoy.

Remember your first coffee? Beer? Cocktail? Chances are, "first was worst." You stuck with it—added cream and sugar, tried a different brand, maybe a different mixer—perfectly acceptable practices to learn taste preferences.

Wine trials are the same. Add sparkling water for a spritzer. Mull it like apple cider for a warm winter beverage. Cook with wine. There are no rules to exploring the various flavor profiles. Mental notes help: Do you prefer sweet or dry? White or red? Mixed with something or all by itself?

One of life's great pleasures, every wine journey begins somewhere. No one starts as an expert, a connoisseur; so relax. Explore wine at your own pace, in your own way, without fear or intimidation.

Don't be embarrassed by the term *newbie*. Own it! Everyone starts as a newbie, even experts. Most experts enjoy sharing personal experiences; and, the less you pretend to know, the more information you will receive from any oenophile worth the name (pronounced E-nuh-FILE)—a wine lover; connoisseur—and a word you'll likely never use unless to impress snobby wine folk with your new wine vocabulary.

As with any skill, the more fundamentals you understand, the more you can customize preferences. Learn to taste and enjoy wine and choose confidently when purchasing.

This book strips away pretentious wine-speak and provides no-nonsense information in easy-to-navigate sections. You'll explore:

- Major types of grapes and wine styles
- Which grapes grow where, or TERROIR (pronounced tay-WAHR)
- How wine is made—just the basics
- How to choose on more than price alone
- Practical advice on tasting, drinking, and serving

Be confident. Most of the fun in drinking wine comes from crafting and sharing your opinions, while honoring others' rights to their own. Your palate shifts with time, as do your preferences.

Most wine journeys start with lighter, food-friendly **WHITES** and **ROSÉS** (pronounced ro-ZAYZ, fancy-speak for "pinks"); eventually, some discover bolder, heavier **REDS** and never drink pinks again. **SPARKLING** and **DESSERT** wines attract loyal fans, but aren't for everyone. Just as you've adjusted your coffee preference (or decided you're really a tea person), you won't know until you try.

Wine should neither be feared nor revered, but drunk and enjoyed. Embrace the fun; discover which wines you prefer drinking with food and which ones sans nibbles. Boldly explore all styles: light, dark, sweet, dry, fruity, sparkling, and aromatic. It's a game, not a contest. Be as picky or adventurous as you like.

Congratulations—you now know the five main categories of wine:

1. White
2. Rosé
3. Red
4. Sparkling (Champagne)
5. Dessert (Sweet)

Cheers to starting on your connoisseur's path!

"Wine is sunlight, held together by water."
—GALILEO, ASTRONOMER AND FATHER OF MODERN SCIENCE

Wine Today

HOW WE GOT HERE

*W*ine's first-recorded origins, in the vicinity of Persia (modern-day Iran), hover between 6,000 and 5,000 BC. Ever since, wine has been made from tree fruits, berries, flowers, and grains (such as rice). Fermentation allowed longer storage, and the alcohol prevented growth of unfriendly bacteria, mold, and microorganisms. Ancient Egyptian paintings demonstrate entire wine-making processes, specifically using grapes. Even storage vessels in Egyptian royal burial chambers display the types of grapes they contained and the years they were harvested.

In 4,000 BC the Greeks stepped up, inventing the grape press and medicinal wine. By 3,000 BC, wine drinking was spreading fast: to modern-day Italy, southern France, Spain, Portugal, and northern Africa. Greek wine was heavy, sweet, and syrupy. Diluting it with sea water by cooking or by adding fruit and spices rendered it quaffable.

A few centuries later, the Romans took note, establishing grape-growing throughout Europe, developing TRELLISING (growing grapevines up off the ground), and becoming the first master COOPERS (wooden barrel makers)—abandoning clay storage jars forever. Wooden barrels are important for aging. Roman records confirm they were the first to consume barrels of wine up to a century after harvest. The wine world never looked back.

Around the eleventh century CE, Europe's political turmoil spurred the transfer of vineyard stewardship to politically neutral monasteries. With a propensity for agriculture, monks enjoyed advantageous circumstances for consuming, distributing, and selling the resulting wines. Thus, monasteries became centers of commerce, spurring the evolution of villages—which became thriving towns and, eventually, cities.

By the 1800s, wine appreciation had advanced substantially. Once the wealthy began buying vineyards, labels were born to showcase glamorous estate holdings under family names. (Wine was not typically labeled before.)

By 1900, a nasty parasite stowaway, phylloxera, crossing the Atlantic aboard an American merchant ship, wiped out most of Europe's vineyards. This forced the eventual mash-up of Old World winemakers into New World vineyards across the Americas, Australia, and South Africa. Customs were transferred, methods were adapted, technologies were created—changing wine landscapes forever.

America's reputation for "plonk"—overly sweet, low-quality, cheap wine—can be traced back to Prohibition, when drinkers were conditioned to the taste of homemade wines, oversweetened to disguise flaws.

US servicemen returning home from the World Wars brought a new taste for refined wines, creating true market opportunity for a United States wine industry. The Americans—always the rebels—named wines for the primary grape used, unlike the European tradition of naming by region of origin. Following this, US wines finally blew open the doors to international credibility. In the now-famous Judgment of Paris (1976), nine French judges unwittingly awarded first place to both a California Chardonnay and a Cabernet Sauvignon, beating their own reigning world-champion wines. US innovation in viticulture continues to lead the industry today.

"Most of us start our serious education in wine-tasting when we begin to wonder, 'What is it about this wine that makes me like it?' As we expand our knowledge … and come to understand why certain wines are pleasing and others are not, we are increasingly able to make refined, consistent judgments of taste and informed wine purchases."

—MARIAN W. BALDY, PhD,
WINE EDUCATOR AND AUTHOR

Ten Interesting Facts About Wine Production

FROM SOIL TO HARVEST

1. Grapes are the only self-contained fruit with all three ingredients required to ferment into an alcoholic beverage that resists spoilage—sugar, acid/tannins, and natural yeast.

2. A grapevine cutting from a parent plant can be planted by itself as a **CLONE** or **GRAFTED** onto another grapevine of a different variety and still produce its own kind.

3. Don't enjoy wet socks on your feet? Neither do grapevines. They prefer light or rocky soils that drain well and don't waterlog their roots.

4. Climate influences grape quality more than the soil.

5. Vineyards do best between 30-degree and 50-degree latitudes: winters cold enough to sleep without getting frostbite (winterkill); but summer suns not hot enough to "bake" them.

6. *Terroir* does not mean "soil"—it combines every growing condition: soil properties, topography, slope direction, rainfall, temperature, humidity, wind, fog, and matching the right grape variety to its preferred conditions.

7. A growing season consists of five stages:

   Dormancy: winter

   Budbreak: between February and April, when small flowers and leaves appear on vines

Bloom: eight weeks after budbreak, when fertilized flowers become grape berries

Veraison: eight to ten weeks after bloom, when grapes begin to swell and change color

Harvest: six to ten weeks after veraison

8. More wine labels say "made from organically grown grapes" than "organic" because organic grape-growing is still expensive and higher-maintenance, but wines labeled "organic" both require organic grapes and prohibit sulfites (regularly used to preserve color and fruit aromas).

9. Flowering plants planted at the end of grapevine rows are used as early indicators for pest or disease.

10. Wine caves hold a constant temperature of 59 degrees Fahrenheit with consistent humidity, reducing evaporation and the need for costly air-conditioning.

"As you learn more about wine—how it looks, how it smells, how it tastes—some of the mystery that surrounds it disappears, but none of the romance."

—YVONNE RICII,
WINE EDUCATOR AND AUTHOR

WORLD OF WINE

WINE REGIONS AROUND THE WORLD

Less ▬▬▬▬▬▬ More
Yearly Production

MIGRATION OF GRAPE PRODUCTION

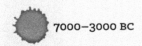 7000–3000 BC

 3000 BC–0

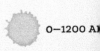 0–1200 A

1200—1500 AD   1500—1900 AD   1900—PRESENT

Future Developments in Wine Making

Puns aside, important shifts are bubbling in the wine industry. Global competition delivers consistency and better prices, but multinational corporations gobbling up mom-and-pop boutiques threaten variety.

Global warming and drought affect land costs, crop yields, and water issues in some giant regions (California); meanwhile, some areas are experiencing record production increases (e.g., Oregon and Washington).

Tourism continues to create its love-hate byproducts: threatening overdevelopment of formerly idyllic areas, overt marketing of cultures, and the disappearance of traditions. Even the way wines are made is changing.

FLAVORS AND STYLES

Acidic wines complement food, so sommeliers choose them for restaurant lists. Add to that the exploding craft beer and cocktail trends, and the result is that casual diners nowadays try the bolder, more unique wines offered.

NEW WORLD BOOM

Australia, New Zealand, South America, South Africa, and Asia are all investing heavily in new wine exports.

TECHNOLOGICAL "PERFECTION"

Flavor profiles are changing—vineyard software can now transmit precise information for each vine. In nature, uniform ripeness isn't possible.

ENVIRONMENT

Screw caps (replacing the declining cork tree) and plastic containers are slowly making inroads in Western Europe and the United States, but organic farming and sustainability are taking hold globally.

"Great wine is about nuance, surprise, subtlety, expression, qualities that keep you coming back for another taste. Rejecting a wine because it is not big enough is like rejecting a book because it is not long enough, or a piece of music because it is not loud enough."

KERMIT LYNCH
ADVENTURES ON THE WINE ROUTE

WORLD'S MOST POPULAR VARIETALS

GRAPE VARIETAL	COUNTRY OF ORIGIN	TYPE
Arneis	Italy: Piedmont	White
Cava	Spain	White, Sparkling
Chardonnay	US: CA, OR; Australia; New Zealand	White
Pinot Grigio	Italy: Tre Vinezie	White
Prosecco	Italy: Veneto	White, Sparkling
Riesling	Australia; Austrian; France: Alsace; Germany	White
Sauvignon Blanc	Austria; US: CA; New Zealand: Marlborough; South Africa	White
Vinho Verde	Portugal: Minho	White
Barbera	Italy: Piedmont	Red
Cabernet Sauvignon	US: CA, WA; Australia; Chile; Italy; South Africa	Red
Carmenère	Chile: Central Valley	Red
Malbec	Argentina: Mendoza	Red
Merlot	US: CA, WA; Chile	Red
Pinot Noir	US: CA, OR; France: Burgundy	Red
Shiraz	Australia; South Africa	Red
Syrah	France: Rhone; US: WA	Red
Zinfandel	US: CA	Red

WORLD'S MOST POPULAR BLENDS

BLENDED WINES	REGION OF ORIGIN	GRAPES USED
Bordeaux	France: Bordeaux	Red: Cabernet Sauvignon, Merlot, Cabernet Franc, Petit Verdot, Malbec
Bourgogne/ Burgundy	France: Burgundy	Red: Pinot Noirs & White: Chardonnays
Champagne	France: Champagne	Sparkling White: each one uses 30–60 still wines, usually Chardonnay
Vins de Pays d'Oc	France: Languedoc-Roussillon	White & Red: Labeled single varietal but combine many vineyards for Cabernet, Chardonnay, Merlot, Sauvignon Blanc, Syrah
Pouilly-Fumé, Sancerre, Vouvray	France: Loire	White & Red: Chardonnay, Sauvignon Blanc, Cabernet, Gamay, Pinot Noir
Châteauneuf-du-Pape, Côtes-du-Rhône, Other Rhônes	France: Rhone	Red: Syrah, Grenache, Mourvèdre
Barbarescos & Barolos	Italy: Piedmont	Red: Two different red wines from same grape, Nebbiolo
Chianti, "Super Tuscans"	Italy: Tuscany	Red: Sangiovese
Port	Portugal: Douro	Fortified, Red: See page
Priorat	Spain: Priorat	Red: Garnacha, Cariñena, Cabernet Sauv, Merlot, Syrah
Rioja	Spain: Rioja	Red: Tempranillo, Graciano, Garnacha

BILLIONS OF LITERS*
CONSUMED PER COUNTRY

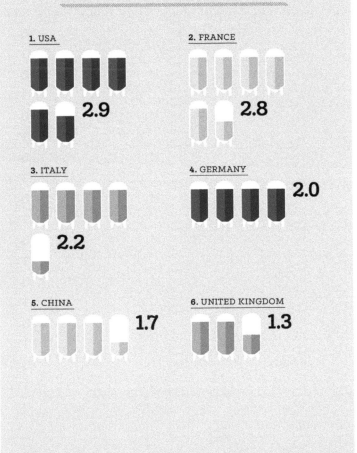

1. USA

2.9

2. FRANCE

2.8

3. ITALY

2.2

4. GERMANY

2.0

5. CHINA

1.7

6. UNITED KINGDOM

1.3

*VOLUME CONSUMED DURING 2013   = 0.5 BILLION LITERS

LITERS CONSUMED
PER CAPITA, GLOBALLY

1. VATICAN CITY

73.8

2. ANDORRA

46.4

3. FRANCE

44.2

4. SAINT-PIERRE
AND MIQUELON

43.6

5. SLOVENIA

43.3

6. CROATIA

42.6

7. MACEDONIA

41.5

8. PORTUGAL

40.9

9. SWITZERLAND

40.4

10. NORFOLK ISLAND

39.9

56. USA

10.4

= 5 LITERS

Enjoying Wine

TASTING VERSUS DRINKING

The most intimidating aspect of buying or ordering wine is the overwhelming variety of choices. Tasting is essential. The drinking part is easy, once you know what you like. Tasting involves five "S" steps, in this order:

SEE, SWIRL, SMELL, SIP, SWALLOW

How to Taste

Before that first taste, consider potential environmental offenders affecting your experience: overpowering scents, smoke, cologne, glassware detergent, and even plastic odors in cups or drinking vessels. Make sure no chewing gum, mints, or strong flavors are lingering in your mouth. Cleanse a tainted palate with neutral flavors. Water, bread, or crackers are topmost among these.

SEE

Hold the glass by the stem, tilt it slightly away from you (the best vantage point), then look at the wine through the glass. Experts can judge age by color. You can't *yet*, but you can certainly recognize "light or dark," "bright or deep," "clear or cloudy." If bubbly, what size are the bubbles and how fast are they moving? Every visual cue sends messages to the brain about what you will taste.

SWIRL

Swirling aerates the wine, incorporating air to "open up" the flavors. When bottled, wine is squeezed into its Sunday best but, in a glass, it prefers loungewear; so give it a twirl to unwind. Only swirl wines without bubbles.

Start by placing the glass on the table, your hand flat on the base of the glass, and guide it in a circular motion to gently swish the liquid around the glass.

Then you can practice raising the glass by the stem or base, without the aid of a hard surface, and create the circular motions with your wrist and forearm.

SMELL

Now that you've aerated your wine, introduce your nose to its new friend. Bring the wine glass up to your face; don't be shy—place your nose right in the opening. Inhale fairly deeply.

As you identify (silently) immediate scents, hold them in your head for a second. Use "OAB" (off-odors, aroma, bouquet) as a mental checklist you will come back to time and again.

"O" stands for OFF-ODORS. Trust your nose—it knows. Unpleasant smells usually mean unpleasant tastes (though you might occasionally be surprised, as with cheese). However, smelling burned matches, wet cardboard, basement mildew, or nail polish remover means actual flaws—rare, but possible. If detected, alert your server to verify your discovery, or recork the wine and set it aside to return to the retailer.

"A" stands for AROMA. If wine were pizza, aroma would mean each *individual* ingredient your nose picks up: yeasty, toasty bread; tangy tomato; fresh basil; melty cheese. In wine-speak, aroma comes from the grapes and can be citrusy, woody, fruity, nutty. With experience, those descriptors get even more specific: Citrusy becomes grapefruit; woody becomes cedar; fruity becomes berry; nutty becomes almond; and so on. The more wine you drink, the more grape characteristics you recognize.

"B" stands for BOUQUET. Now it's personal. As in a pizza, "bouquet" means "the sum of its parts": margherita or pepperoni, or pineapple and ham, etc. Think: grapes plus aging plus other nuances, combined. Your favorite Chardonnay boasts an immediately recognizable bouquet of vanilla, almond, and tropical fruit, luring you in, making you salivate in anticipation.

Note: One does not dissect these split-second thoughts out loud. Think of it like this: When someone mentions a band, the genre, image, style, and sound quality are immediately conjured into one fleeting thought. Each individual musician and instrument is not explicitly inventoried every time you talk about the band.

SEE. HOLD GLASS BY STEM AT SLIGHT ANGLE. LOOK AT COLOR AND CLARITY AGAINST A LIGHT BACKGROUND.

SWIRL. HOLD GLASS BY THE BASE AND SWIRL ON A SURFACE (OR IN THE AIR) TO AERATE SLIGHTLY.

SMELL. DO YOU NOTICE OFF-ODORS? WHAT AROMAS
CAN YOU IDENTIFY IN THE BOUQUET?

WHAT ARE BLIND TASTINGS?

In **BLIND TASTINGS**, the drinker does not know or cannot see which wines are being served. This is the opposite of an **OPEN TASTING**, where drinkers are aware of which wines are being poured to taste. Blind tastings are the best way to form opinions about which wines you truly enjoy because outside influences, such as preconceived ideas or information are removed and you only concentrate on taste and subjective experience.

Continuing the band example, the concept of **BALANCE** is similar: We all have opinions about bands that play well together versus bands dominated by one person. As wine, the latter would be considered unbalanced. When wine **AROMAS** work together, the bouquet announces its potential balance. But if one aroma really sticks out, the bouquet indicates it might be unbalanced. That doesn't mean "bad," per se, but a Sauvignon Blanc smelling primarily of grapefruit will probably taste that way, too. So you'd better like grapefruit.

SIP

Sipping confirms whether your aroma/bouquet assumptions are true. Sip enough wine to move it around in your mouth. Take your time. Pay attention. What do you taste? Do the flavors match its aromas and bouquet? What parts of your mouth and tongue pick up the flavors? Do you detect sweet? Tart? Creamy? Crisp? Bitter? Do flavors linger? (If so, where?)

SWALLOW

What happens once it is down the hatch? Sipping activates different "flavor zones" on your tongue (sweet, sour, salty, bitter). What you taste after you swallow is called the finish. The lingering flavor essences provide length. Each style will remind you of specific flavors, so remember tastes you find pleasing. This is the easiest way to add wines to your repertoire.

Food also affects a wine's taste. A tart, dry wine that's hard to drink on its own may pair well with food, because contrast makes flavors pop. On the flip side, a usually delicious fruity, dry red you love by itself would fight with a mouthful of fried pickles, making both unappealing.

Don't second-guess your own vocabulary. Professionals know helpful wine-speak translations. Just remember, the cardinal rule is: always drink what you like, and like what you drink.

TERMS TO KNOW

ACID: Naturally occurring. Vital. Adds a fresh, crisp taste.

AROMA: Each individual ingredient your nose picks up.

BALANCE: When a wine's flavors, textures, and bouquet complement each other. No single aroma or component overpowers any other.

BLEND: A wine featuring multiple grape varieties; not intended as a single varietal.

BOUQUET: The sum of the wine's parts.

DEPTH: Complex or rich flavors. The opposite of lean, flat, or thin.

FORWARD FRUIT: The first, most-prominent flavor is pronounced fruit instead of a complex range of flavors.

PALATE: Ability to dissect and identify impressions (tastes, smells) when eating or drinking.

TABLE WINE: Normal, still (not sparkling) wine. Standard blends for food and everyday drinking.

TANNINS: Exist naturally in grape skins and seeds, producing "pucker" taste perceived as dry; prominent in red wines.

TERROIR **(TAY-WAHR):** Each region's geography, soil types, and climate that determine the unique flavors the grapes from that location develop, and which grapes grow best there.

VARIETAL: Wines made with a majority of a specific grape variety. Each state and country has different minimum requirements. For example: The United States requires a wine to have at least 75 percent-plus of a grape variety to be called that varietal on the label. Oregon requires 90 percent.

VARIETY: A particular type of grape, e.g., Cabernet Sauvignon, Chardonnay, etc.

VITIS VINIFERA: Grapes specifically for making wine, not eating.

REAL-WORLD WORDS FOR DESCRIBING TASTE VERSUS FANCY TERMS

GRAPE VARIETY	REAL-WORLD TERMS	FANCY TERMS
Chardonnay, White	Buttery Citrus or tropical fruits Oaky Rich Smooth texture Vanilla	Aromatic versus dumb Butterscotch Complex Lactic Pencil shavings Tobacco
Sauvignon Blanc, White	Austere Crisp Grapefruit Green apple Having aromas of fresh herbs Refreshing Tart	Agreeable Gooseberry Herbaceous Lively Mineral-y Passion fruit Tartaric Herbaceous
Champagne or Sparkling, White and Rosé	"A lot going on" Bread or toast Delicate Fizzy Floral Fruity Sweet	Apple, citrus, strawberry, etc. Complex Elegant Perfumed Prickly Sweet, dry, clean, fresh Yeasty
Pinot Noir, Red	Barnyard Drying Earthy Fruity Medium Smoky Smooth	Astringent Bacon fat Cherry, cranberry, raspberry, rhubarb, etc. Cigar box Forest floor Refined Silky

GRAPE VARIETY	REAL-WORLD TERMS	FANCY TERMS
Sangiovese, Red	Astringent Having flavors or aromas of spices like cinnamon, cloves, or pepper Intense Nutty Savory Tree fruits	Almond Black cherry, sour cherry, plums Herbal, leather, cedar Muscular Spicy Tannic
Cabernet Sauvignon, Red	Berries Big and powerful Full-bodied Herbaceous Vegetative Velvety (tannins) Woody	Balanced tannins Blackberry, blackcurrant, plum, etc. Fleshy, round Green pepper, black olive, violets Licorice, mint Robust or aggressive Sawdust, pencil shavings, cigar box, tobacco

"I shall drink no wine before its time.
OK, it's time!"

—GROUCHO MARX,
COMEDIAN AND FILM STAR

Temperature, Wine Breathing, and Decanting

TEMPERATURE

The rule "serve whites cold; reds at room temperature" is misleading. Refrigerator-cold (below 40 degrees Fahrenheit) temperatures suppress delicate aromatics, rendering lean wines thin or metallic; and "room temperature" historically referred to earlier times when there were no thermostats.

The correct temperature targets for serving are:

- Lean whites, such as Pinot Grigio: 42 to 46 degrees Fahrenheit
- Full-bodied whites, such as Chardonnay: 48 to 52 degrees Fahrenheit
- All reds should be somewhere in the 58 to 65 degrees Fahrenheit range, not 70-plus degrees Fahrenheit

WINE BREATHING AND DECANTING

Wine flavors open up once mixed with air (remember swirling?). Open wine one to two hours before serving and pre-pour into glasses, or DECANT, to expose the wine to air. Undesirable compounds evaporate from the wine before affecting the fruit.

Decanting is breathing on steroids. To do so, transfer a bottle of wine into a larger, more open container (see Decanting, page 60).

TIPS & TRICKS TO IMPROVE
OR DIMINISH TASTE

ARTICHOKES, ASPARAGUS, AND SALAD POSE CHALLENGES. When dressed with vinegar, forgo wine until the next course. You'll enjoy the wine so much more with food not prepared with vinegar—your wine will not compete unpleasantly for your mouth's attention. Bright, citrusy whites work well when served with fats like creamy sauces or dressings, cheese, dairy, eggs, cured meats, and oils.

APPLES, BERRIES, AND CITRUS MATCH MANY WINE AROMAS, so pair with a like ingredient, i.e., green apple-y Riesling with a dish containing green apples. Tart fruit balances sweet wine, and vice versa. If citrus zest is used, avoid dry wines, but fruity wines pop from the acid in the peels.

TAME SPICY PEPPERS with sweet or fruity wines and creamy whites.

BEWARE OF SALT AND WALNUTS— both exaggerate tannin bitterness. Salty-food people tend to prefer whites; walnuts work best with dessert wines.

"When in doubt, bring bubbles out!"

Types of Wine

The Big Five, in Order

WHITE

White wines are made from green grapes that are crushed, pressed, and skinned before fermenting in big stainless steel vats or wooden barrels. White wines are often cold-stabilized before bottling, meaning chilled in huge tanks to prevent naturally occurring crystals from forming. (If you see crystals in the bottle or on the cork, know they are harmless.) Colors range from translucent to light greens and yellows to deep golden-yellow, and cover all ranges from dry to sweet and light to heavy.

ROSÉ (PINKS AND BLUSH WINES)

To make pink wine (even pink "bubbles"), the winemaker has two simple choices: Leave the skins of red grapes on during pressing or fermentation until sufficiently pink; or add red wine into the white juice to achieve the desired pinkness. Rosés are light, fruity, and best served cool. They typically go great with warm-weather al fresco dining.

RED

Red wines come from red, purple, and black grapes. Crushed before fermentation, their skins are left on to ferment with the juice in either steel tanks or wooden barrels. Afterward, the mash is pressed again to help extract the distinct colors from the skins. Aging longer than whites helps soften tannins and develop structure. Colors range from intense purples to ruby or brick reds. Tastes range from dry to sweet, thin to full-bodied, and they have light to heavy tannins.

CHAMPAGNE ("BUBBLES," "FIZZ," SPARKLING, CAVA, PROSECCO, SEKT)

Dom Pérignon, a monk, gets credit for Champagne, but his actual claim to fame has to do with blending wines from different places and making white wine out of red-skinned grapes. Champagne production still uses both methods, but SECOND FERMENTATION, mastered in the 1700s, elevates our favorite fizz to today's celebrated status. Grapes are picked, juiced, and fermented separately by vineyard or lot. Later, blending achieves a signature wine style. This blended result then gets a nice second dose of sugar, plus new yeast that promptly stuff their microscopic faces with the sugar Thanksgiving-style, burping out carbon dioxide bubbles that remain forever trapped in the final juice.

SWEET WINES

Dessert wines taste sweeter because they are made with sweeter fruit: In all cases, grapes are left on vines longer so that their sugars become more concentrated (see Sweet Wines, page 63).

"Most white wines are bottled three and twelve months after harvest. Bottling of red wines is rarely done within a year."

—RICHARDS LYON,
VINE TO WINE

Regions and Profiles

These brief highlights will help you navigate retail shelves or any wine list:

UNITED STATES

- **CALIFORNIA:** Napa Valley, known worldwide for Cabernet Sauvignons. Sonoma, recognized for Pinot Noir and Chardonnay. Inland regions produce great Zinfandels.
- **OREGON:** Burgundian winemakers have cultivated best-in-class Pinot Noirs.
- **WASHINGTON:** Rhône varietals are superstars; juicy Syrahs.

FRANCE

- *VIN ORDINAIRE* is 85 percent of all everyday-drinking French table wine.
- **AOC** (Appellation d'Origine Contrôlée) covers the remaining 15 percent of complex wines meeting strict standards.
- **ALSACE:** Same grapes as Germany, but French methods produce drier Rieslings, Gewürztraminers, and Pinot Blancs than its neighbor's sweeter versions.
- **BORDEAUX:** Regarded as the finest reds in the world, from only five grape varieties allowed; age well; named after château of grapes' source.
- **BURGUNDY:** World's most elegant Pinot Noirs and Chardonnays. Beaujolais.

- **CHAMPAGNE**: World's best sparkling wines from Pinot Noir and Chardonnay grapes.
- **RHÔNE VALLEY**: All Syrah-based (Côte Rhôtie, Hermitage—add Grenache grapes for Châteauneuf-du-Pape).

ITALY

Here you'll find the world's heaviest wine drinkers—even beating the French! Almost every corner produces wine, favoring reds. Sangiovese and Nebbiolo shine.

SOUTH AMERICA

- **ARGENTINA**: reds, mostly concentrated on quantity. Great values.
- **CHILE**: reds, mostly concentrated on quality.

AUSTRALIA

- **CABERNET** and **SHIRAZ** (pronounced sh-RAZZ, not sh-RAHZ) rule the reds.
- **SÉMILLON, CHARDONNAY**, and **RIESLINGS** rule the whites.

SPAIN

- **RIOJA** and **TEMPRANILLO** like Spain's rocky, arid, hot climes.
- **SHERRY** will always be a unique mainstay.

UNITED STATES WINE LABEL WITH EXPLANATION

① *Vintage 918*

② CABERNET SAUVIGNON

⑦ 2012

RED WINE
④ 13.5% ALC./VOL.   750 ml   **⑥** NAPA VALLEY

Vintage 918

③ Bottled by 918 Parker Street, Berkeley CA 94710
Cabernet Sauvignon
Contains sulfites
750 Ml

⑤

GOVERNMENT WARNING: (1) according to the surgeon general, women should not drink alcoholic beverages during pregnancy because of the risk of birth defects. (2) Consumption of alcoholic beverages impairs your ability to drive a car or operate machinery, and may cause health problems.

In the United States, a wine label must contain seven items:

1. Brand name
2. Wine class or type (is it a varietal, blend, or what grapes were used?)
3. Name and address of bottler
4. Alcohol content
5. Sulfite statement/health warning/net content
6. Appellation of origin, or where the grapes were grown
7. Vintage date, when grapes were harvested, not when the wine was bottled

Varietal, Appellation, Vineyard Designation, and Vintage

VARIETAL

Where and how people grow up influences their tastes, styles, personalities, and so on. Wine grapes are no different. The same grape variety planted in different *terroir* may possess similarities, but a Chardonnay grape from sunny Sonoma, California, will taste different than the same grape grown in Burgundy, France.

A grape cannot be named the varietal on the label unless a minimum required amount of only that grape was used to make that wine. Requirements change based on location. In California, our sunny Sonoma Chardonnay can be labeled as such as long as 75 percent of its grapes were Chardonnay from Sonoma. If the winemaker used less than 75 percent Sonoma Chardonnay—even Chardonnay from elsewhere in California—that wine only qualifies as a California Chardonnay because the Sonoma minimum was not met. In Oregon, wines require 90 percent of a grape variety to qualify as a varietal. And don't even get started on France—they label varietals similarly by location, not grape varieties.

APPELLATION

Appellation describes a more specific place of origin. If someone mentions they live in New York City, and someone else mentions Manhattan, and the third says the East Village, each is providing more specific information about the same area.

Wine drinkers frequently recognize appellations and begin to understand nuances to seek out new wines from similar areas. Appellations can be the name of a country, state, county, or geographic region, like a mountain range or valley.

VINEYARD DESIGNATION

A **VINEYARD DESIGNATION**, by comparison, is one step narrower—all grapes used in the wine are required to be grown in that vineyard. For example: The Smiths love Spring Mountain Cabernets, a famous Napa appellation. Their local shop sells three Spring Mountain Cabernets, meaning three cabernet varietals from the Spring Mountain appellation. One bottle's label adds the line "Wurtele Vineyard." This vineyard designation means the grapes only came from the Wurtele Vineyard. Wines using mostly one type of grape from only one vineyard are referred to as *single-vineyard varietals*. They have limited availability, are premium quality, and, therefore, more expensive.

VINTAGE

When a vintage year is given on a label, 85 percent of the wine must be from grapes from that year's growth. If no vintage is present, multiple years' harvests were combined to make that wine.

Composition

Our ABCs provide the structure and foundation for words and language. Likewise, wine's "ABTs" provide the foundation for a wine's structure: acidity, astringency, bitterness, body, and tannins. Each structural component has a role in achieving balance.

ACIDITY

Acidity is important. Too much tastes like vinegar; too little makes a wine boring. Acid makes wine bright and lively on the tongue. Consider how a mere squirt of lemon elevates a glass of water. Adding the juice of a full lemon, though, converts the flavor to tart, or possibly sour. Adding sugar and ice results in lemonade, which may be sharp and zesty, or even sweet, depending on how the acid and sugar are balanced.

As a rule, white wines showcase more acid than reds. The same idea applies to apples: The tart "zing" of a Granny Smith is clearly more acidic than the sweet flavor of a Red Delicious. Tart flavors activate the middle-tongue flavor zone on either side closest to the teeth. Different people appreciate different levels of acidity, so what is pleasing to one may not be to another.

ASTRINGENCY

Astringency is the effect perceived as drying or puckering. Tannins, the primary cause, come from the astringent portions of grapes: skins, seeds, and stems. If you've ever chewed a grape seed and experienced that "strong black tea" sensation (mouth puckering, "dry" tongue), that's it. These tannins prolong aging and add complexity.

SULFITES WARNINGS

WHAT DOES THE SULFITES WARNING ON ALMOST EVERY WINE LABEL MEAN?

The sulfites warning is the wine-world's equivalent to government-mandated peanut warnings on food labels—even though applicable to only a very small percentage of people who are extremely sensitive or allergic to sulfites (or steroid-dependent asthmatics). Sulfites are added in production to prevent oxidation and inhibit microbial activity. While rare, too much sulfite in wine is detected as a "burned matchstick" characteristic.

BITTERNESS AND BODY

Bitterness applies to flavors typically associated with leafy greens: kale, chard, funky salads. The back of the tongue toward the throat is primarily where we detect bitter tastes. Chomp on rhubarb, then take a sip of that lemon water from earlier and you'll quickly notice where acidity versus bitterness activates your tongue.

The second "B" stands for "body." An abstract concept, the best way to think of a wine's body is to consider the range of professional words used to describe it: empty, thin, narrow, light, lean, stringy, medium, sinewy, ample, muscular, full, thick, heavy, rich, or robust. Drinking wine trains your palate to recognize and categorize subjective differences in how they feel in your mouth. For example, ice tea is "lean;" Thai-style ice tea (with sweet cream) is "rich."

TANNINS

Tannins are essential to structure, especially in reds. They impart that silky, smooth texture in an elegant, aged wine. With age, tannins "mellow" by forming longer chains that won't slip into your tongue's crevasses as you drink. This imparts satiny smoothness as opposed to puckering astringency. Tannin vocabulary may clarify the effect on your mouth: light, soft, smooth, velvety, balanced, integrated, dusty, powdery, chalky, drying, green, stalky, or woody. Finally, tannins can also be described in terms of qualities such as aggressive, hard, heavy, or persistent.

DRYNESS

Dryness applies to the wine's finish, but many factors affect the perception of whether a wine is dry or sweet. Dryness results when most or all of the sugar in the wine has been converted to alcohol. Acidity, astringency, bitterness, body, and tannins all combine to exaggerate drying effects on the palate. High alcohol levels also contribute dryness, also called "heat."

The upshot is, the better a wine's structure, the better it ages and the longer it takes to break down over time.

BALANCE

Balance summarizes how all components work together. When "out of balance," a wine's parts are not working together—the "terrible toos": too sweet, too acidic, too many tannins, too much oak, too much alcohol, etc.

BOUQUET + ABTS + DRYNESS + STRUCTURE = BALANCE

WINE COMPOSITION: EXAMPLES OF OPPOSING STRUCTURE DESCRIPTORS

IS IT . . .	OR?	IS IT . . .	OR?
Formless	Consistent	Hollow	Full or Solid
Flat	Layered	Attenuated	Seamless
Angular	Round	Disjointed	Elegant, Finesse
Short	Long	Tight	Open

Coloration (with Age)

Clear and bright is always preferred to cloudy and hazy, with the exception of unfiltered or organic wines. Color variations provide important distinctions about taste and age. In general, pale or green-tinged whites hail from cool climates and are crisp. Golden wines such as barrel-oaked whites are more deeply colored and come from warmer climes, implying a more round and sensuous wine. White wines darken with age. Avoid tinges of brown, as they are usually oxidizing beyond the acceptable range. (Exceptions are fortified or dessert wines.)

Red wines' colors give away more information. Starting at deep purple-red, these wines range from ruby to brick red to tawny. Molecules bond and fall to the bottom, creating sediment as wine ages. Sediment contains pigment, so greater age equals less color intensity (the barrel wood absorbs color, too). Wines intended to age well start out as deeply intense purple-reds, an indication of a high concentration of grape skin pigments used in the early stages of production to provide tannins, the building blocks for structure and age. Red wines aged in their bottles keep their color longer.

COLOR INTENSITY

To judge a wine's age, look at the wine in the glass: Examine the wine from the edge to the center. The more pale (or brownish) the rim and edge are compared to the concentration or intensity of the center color, the more mature the wine.

YOUNG WINE   MATURE WINE

Winemaking

The Process

Wine is just fermented grape juice. Knowing which grape juice you like, what fermentation you prefer, whether you enjoy grapes from specific places or a particular winery (or person), goes a long way towards finding wines you enjoy purchasing and drinking.

Once grapes are picked, or harvested, they are taken to a winery as quickly as possible. Grapes are pressed or crushed, and nature takes over.

Wine starts as sugar and yeast. The grapes already contain both—sugar on the inside, wild yeast on the outside. When mushed, pressed, and left to ferment, the yeast starts consuming all the sugars in the juice. The results are alcohol and carbon dioxide. Winemakers manipulate the mixture and leave it in vessels to age. When the desired results are achieved, they bottle the wine, cork it, and let it age longer, depending on the end goal.

WINEMAKING PROCESS

HARVEST
FALL: GRAPES PICKED, PEAK
'HANGTIME'.

SORT:
GRAPES SORTED;
TRANSPORTED TO WINERY.

GREEN GRAPES (WHITE WINE):
CRUSHED ➤ PRESSED ➤
FERMENTED

RED GRAPES (RED WINE):
CRUSHED ➤ **FERMENTED** ➤
PRESSED

BARREL AGING (OPTIONAL):
COMPLEX WINES FILTERED
('FINED') AND AGED LONGER IN
OAK BARRELS.

FILL BOTTLES

CORK OR
CLOSURE
ADDED

FOIL OR
PLASTIC SEALS

LABEL ADDED

REWARD!

Fermentation

Fermentation starts in the vineyard by winemakers manipulating grapevines to produce specific acid and sugar levels by harvest. Also, pulp and skin proportions determine how much juice, tannin, and color can be extracted from the fruit. Direct or filtered sun on the fruit affects flavors that fermentation will highlight.

Grapes are picked, destemmed, crushed, and pressed in vats as quickly as possible. Nowadays, custom yeast blends are added before the juice is transferred to a fermentation vessel. Temperature control is critical. Similar to the process of smoking meat, "low temperature and slow process" allows the grapes to retain their delicate flavors while preventing oxygen from being introduced, which would destroy the batch.

When the alcohol level reaches 14 to 15 percent, the yeast naturally dies—the same way baking bread kills the yeast in dough. In still wines (without bubbles), the CO_2 gas from fermentation byproducts evaporates through special vents; with Champagne or bubbly, the resulting gas is kept inside the juice.

Oak: Wine's Friend

It was noted previously that it's bad for oxygen to get into wine during fermentation. Well, that's *mostly* true; some level of oxidation is actually desirable. It's just a hassle for most vintners to monitor and manage. Enter the oak barrel—nature's oxygen babysitter.

Most barrels are still made by hand, old school–style via ancient Roman methods. Oak wood, in particular, imparts not only specific desirable flavors and qualities into wine but it is also semipermeable. So, wine won't saturate the wood and leak out, and oxygen can only get in and out in very small quantities—both processes taking place slowly enough to be controlled.

The two main types of oak used are European oak, which imparts distinct rich, toasty vanilla aromas into wines during aging, and American oak which conveys more woodsy flavors. Where oak trees grow influences aromas and flavors that wine-makers can adjust. Coopers also work with winemakers on different wood-seasoning methods: toasting barrel interiors; adding or reducing surface area; even transferring wines between differently aged barrels during aging, since younger barrels have a much stronger influence on flavor.

The small amount of oxygen present in barrel aging actually helps tannin molecules find each other, bond (with other microparticles), and, eventually, settle on the bottom, becoming sediment. Too much oxygen is a bad thing, however, so the space created by the settling of particles or evaporation from the barrel occasionally needs to be filled with more wine from the same lot. This "replacement" wine is designated and reserved specifically for this purpose at the start.

The finest wines in France, and many premium wines in all regions around the globe, are always aged in wood, despite the increasing popularity of stainless steel tank alternatives; even bottle-aging methods are growing in use. While French

DECANTING

Many naturally occurring compounds in wine can inhibit the fruits from shining through when a bottle is first opened. For this reason, decanting is the preferred method of letting undesirables dissipate prior to drinking. Common practice is to decant younger or bolder reds up to 90 minutes prior to serving to intensify their flavor and fruitiness. Bottles older than five years should stand upright for a couple of days prior to drinking to let sediment sink to the bottom. Gently pour the wine into a decanter, being careful to keep the wine sediment-free. (It's harmless, but it tastes gritty and bitter).

winemakers are required to follow many rules (specific grape selections, not adding acids, etc.), they are not required specifically to use French oak barrels for aging.

FLAVOR/CHARACTER

Consider the different flavors oak can impart into different wine styles:

- **SAUVIGNON BLANC:** butterscotch, char, coconut, sawdust, smoke, steel, toast, vanilla
- **CHARDONNAY:** (in addition to those listed for Sauvignon Blanc): almond, baked bread, burned caramel, cashew, cedar, nuts, pencil shavings, tree bark, Vegemite, yogurt
- **CABERNET SAUVIGNON:** (in addition to all the preceding): bacon, burned spice, toffee

Bottling

Finished wines must be intensely double-checked for bottle-readiness because it is hard to correct flaws once bottled. Bottling is tedious, so commercial wineries use large, automated bottling line systems on-site. Small, boutique wineries can bottle by hand or transport wines to a bottling facility.

Sanitized bottles are filled, immediately capped or corked, and then finished with either a foil "capsule" or a dollop of wax. (When opening the wine, capsules need to be peeled off to expose the cork. If waxed, treat the wax as if it isn't there by inserting your corkscrew directly into its surface and twist right down through the wax to extract the cork.) After sealing, bottles are machine-labeled and placed in boxes bottoms-up to keep corks wet, which produces an airtight seal while aging.

This is pretty rough handling, so a few weeks following bottling, wines suffer from **BOTTLE SHOCK** and are left alone to recover body and fruitiness in the stillness of cool, dark cellars or caves. Higher-quality wines will continue aging in their bottles, developing and integrating more flavors while softening tannins.

CONTAINERS: GLASS VERSUS PLASTIC VERSUS BOXES

Once use of clay urns and pots transitioned to glass bottles, glass remained the de facto vessel for long-term storage of finished wines. Sanitized glass imparts no outside tastes or chemicals, and it lasts a very long time.

In France and Australia, bag-in-box combos are much more popular and offer higher-quality wines than typically found in boxed wine in the United States. These containers feature vacuum-sealed bags that deflate as one removes the wine, so the wine does not get exposed to oxygen.

Plastic bottles are growing in popularity due to the environmental/carbon footprint implications of transporting and storing glass. Plastic takes up less room and doesn't break, reducing inventory loss. The trade-off is controversy over whether (or how much of) plastic's microscopic components are absorbed by the wine. Plastic is also permeable, so oxygen is introduced over time, degrading any high-quality or premium wine meant to age. Therefore, while considered "safe," most wines packaged in plastic are meant to be drunk within a year of bottling. "To plastic or not to plastic" is not a cut-and-dried subject. Expect more public debate and experimental packaging on the shelves.

CORK IT! (OR CAP IT?)

Mirroring the plastic versus glass debate, screw caps also have a bit of an image problem when it comes to wine enclosures. Purists have always been staunch supporters of the ubiquitous cork as the one-and-only appropriate enclosure. But nature's resources are finite and may not be able to match increasing global production demands. Natural cork flaws also add potential issues with storage and aging, and can create costly problems. Resulting synthetic plastic corks have become a bridge between tradition and twist-offs.

WATER IN WINE

Three winemakers walk into a bar: an Australian, an American, and a Frenchman . . .

Want to start an instant debate? Mention the topic of water in wine around oenophiles. It boils down to increased "hang time" from modern grape-growing methods in non-European regions. Overripe or super-ripe grapes—depending on one's opinion—tend to result in wines over the 15 percent alcohol limit allowed by European Union importers. Winemakers will sometimes remedy this by incorporating water pre-fermentation, with myriad justifications. The result is not swill, and it is legal (except in the European Union), so it boils down to personal preference.

Enter the screw cap, or twist top: an aluminum lid lined with a food-grade plastic that replaces cork enclosures. Inexpensive and usually effective, many winemakers started using these with whites and wines intended to be consumed within a relatively short timeline (one to two years). But now, more winemakers are using them on all tiers of wines, not just inexpensive ones.

Sweet Wines

Sweet wines are sweeter than table wines because they have either increased natural residual sugar or are FORTIFIED with additional distilled brandy (also made from grapes), which kills the yeast and prevents any more sugar consumption at various stages during fermentation. Normally paired with the cheese or dessert courses, they can also be served on their own as an *aperitif* (before a meal) or a *digestif* (after a meal).

In all cases, the grapes are left on vines longer to elevate their natural sugar levels before harvesting. Then a handful of methods are available to winemakers to intensify complexity and concentrate flavors:

LATE-HARVEST wines are made from grapes left to ripen up to twice as long as when normal grapes would be harvested, thus the name. They are noticeably sweeter right off the vine than grapes used in traditional wines.

NOBLE ROT is a method that uses a safe fungus, *Botrytis cinerea*, to attack grape skins by making holes, causing the grapes to dehydrate, much like raisins. Sauternes are the resulting magical varietal of this process.

German **EISWEIN** and Canadian and American **ICE WINES** are crafted from extra-ripe Riesling grapes left on vines to partially freeze during the first frost. The frozen grapes are immediately picked and pressed to preserve the intense sweet flavors.

FORTIFIED wines include Kir, Vermouth, Madeira, Port, Sherry, and Grappa. Brandy (distilled alcohol also made from grapes) is added at different stages to each, during or after fermentation, which determines whether the wine is sweet or dry. The type of grape, *terroir*, regional traditions, and whether other ingredients are infused will cement each wine's distinct flavor. Many are associated with local customs as to how they are served or used in the preparation of special cuisine.

While PORT is a fortified wine, it is a class unto itself. Only wines from Portugal may be called "port," and there are very specific naming conventions factoring in the fruit, origin, and aging—the youngest being RUBY PORTS, aged up to three years in oak; the oldest being TAWNY PORTS, which can be aged as long as forty or more years. PORT-STYLE refers to any wine of this style that did not originate from Portugal.

Wine Shopping & Storing

Wine Pricing

There is a popular joke around the wine-making world:

Q: How does a winery make $1 million?
A: Start with $5 million and . . .

How much money goes into producing each bottle of wine is a complicated subject. As with any industry, consumers want fair-market opportunity for big guys and boutiques alike. The "big guys" benefit from huge volume discounts all the way up their production and distribution chains, and can pass along cost benefits as consumer savings and affordable pricing. However, some of the kid-glove handling, nuances, personal attention, and human interest stories may get lost in the process. Boutiques and smaller producers bring these advantages to the table, but these allow for less pricing flexibility. One small tweak to their supply chains can have a trickle-down effect on a year's budgets and expenses.

Most people don't consider all of the time and expensive factors that have gone into a bottle they pick up at the store: physical real estate the vineyard grows on; daily vineyard maintenance and management; irrigation and water; staff and labor salaries; harvest;

TIPS FOR CHOOSING GOOD WINE WHEN YOU DON'T KNOW ANYTHING

Know two basics: (1) your budget and (2) whether you want white or red. (Whites are served colder and match more foods.) *Really* new to choosing? Use a $10 target price to eliminate most cheaply made wines. You can go backward into more inexpensive options once you've learned more about your palate.

Wines are usually sorted by geographic origin, so learn which countries make the wines you like. Start there. Later, as you get to know that section of the wine menu, narrow in to different regions of the same country to get a sense of style differences.

For example: "I drink Chianti at my local pizza joint. Italy makes Chianti. Where's the Italy section?" Then try different Chiantis.

Next, graduate to wines made from the same type of grapes, but from different varietals, styles, or countries. If you know Chianti is made from Sangiovese grapes, then consider, what other wines are made from Sangiovese? Any non-Italian ones?

Become a regular at local establishments to build personal rapport with staff who can steer you in helpful directions as you sample. Keep track of favorites and dislikes equally.

transportation; front-to-back wine-making processes; barrels and tanks; storage space; bottling lines; energy costs; labeling, packaging, branding, and marketing; legal compliance, plus state and federal fees; distribution and fulfillment via costly, inefficient three-tier distribution; plus retail education and collateral . . . and that isn't all.

You'll also notice the same bottle of wine costs less at a retail store than in a bar or restaurant. Because profit is the difference between sales and expenses (costs), hospitality businesses closely monitor "pouring costs" to make sure alcoholic beverages contribute a large portion of their revenue to total sales volume. The costs of being able to serve and sell alcohol add up through licensing, taxation, buying appropriate glassware, maintaining proper storage environments, and so on. You are not simply buying the wine, but also paying a premium for the wine-drinking experience, which includes knowledgeable service providing the appropriate conditions and right presentation to maximize the enjoyment of your wine selection.

Whether purchasing from a retailer or dining and drinking establishments, ample choices usually exist in every price bracket to satisfy any palate or budget.

"Good" Versus "Bad" Wines

If the golden rule is "drink what you like and like what you drink," the objective conclusion would be there are no "bad" wines—until you drink one.

Previously, we mentioned potential—but rare—flaws (see page 29) that indicate a wine is bad. But outside of those rare occasions, what makes a wine undesirable? Price is not the only indicator of quality, but it's a fair starting point. Low-quality, "cheap" wines are a combination of the following factors: inexpensive, low-grade grapes; large-scale commercial production methods; accelerated or manipulated aging; oversweetening; bulk packaging for mass retail; flawed or improper handling and storage.

Basically, drinking "swill," "plonk," or a "goon sack" is the equivalent of drinking lemonade made from powder instead of real lemons. Bad wine simply lacks complexity, finesse, or the benefits of time that nature offers. That doesn't mean all inexpensive wines are bad, however. For example, what has been dubbed "Two Buck Chuck," Trader Joe's budget-conscious offering from Charles Shaw Winery, is a notorious top seller. Just remember, inexpensive wine can be cheap *and* good; bad wine is usually just cheap (or cheaply made).

Horizontally or Vertically: How to Store Wine

Wine bottles should be stored *horizontally*, that is, on their side. Keeping the cork in contact with the wine keeps it moist for an airtight seal. Labels should always face up whether you use a box, shelf, specially designed wine rack, or temperature-controlled wine refrigerator. This allows for easy viewing with minimum handling.

The four enemies of wine storage are light, temperature, dry air, and vibration. Many wine rookies stash awkwardly shaped wine

REVIEWING AND POINT SYSTEMS USED FOR EVALUATING WINE

Want to score wine like the pros? Try an "almost official" score card! Real point limits & helpful hints provided for each category:

APPEARANCE	YOUR SCORE
COLOR (Max. 2 points) Depth: Intense = 2; Deep = 1; Faint = 0.	
CLARITY (Max. 1 point) Brilliant = 1; Clear = .5; Dull = 0	
YOUR TOTAL FOR APPEARANCE (3 point maximum)	
NOSE	
INTENSITY (Max. 4) Slight = 0–1; Pleasant = 1–2; Complex = 2–3; Powerful = 4	
NOSE FAULTS (Max. 3) Corky or oxidized = 1-0; Slight = 1–2; No faults = 3	
YOUR TOTAL FOR NOSE (7 point maximum)	
PALATE	
INTENSITY (Max. 3) On a scale of 0–3 points, how do you rate the flavor intensity?	
ACID (Max. 2) Acid too high or low = 0–1; Balanced acid = 2	
PALATE FAULTS (Max. 3) Serious faults = 0–.5; Detectable = 1–2.5; None = 3	
BALANCE (Max. 2) Balanced acid/tannin = 1–1.5; Outstanding = 2	
YOUR TOTAL FOR PALATE (10 point maximum)	
TOTAL MAXIMUM SCORE POSSIBLE: 20.	

SCORING WINE

Gold	18.5 to 20.0 points	Bronze	15.5 to 16.9 points
Silver	17.0 to 18.4 points	Quaffable	14.0 to 15.4 points

racks on top of the refrigerator to save valuable counter space—but you'd be hard-pressed to find a worse location. Kitchens are typically bright and warm, and warm refrigerator generators constantly vibrate. The best storage locations are dark, cool, and still—like closets and basements.

In the wine world, the word "vertical" has a dual meaning: (1) the direction the bottle is placed on the shelf, and (2) a series of the same wine (varietal) from different vintages (years). Retailers sell

COOKING WITH WINE

While inexpensive "cooking wine" is sold as such in grocery stores, use the real thing for best results. Divvy up leftover wine or inexpensive bottles into freezable portions for handy access and use as follows:

1. **DRY RED AND WHITE WINES:** beef stews, cream soups, mussels, clams, and wine-based sauces

2. **DRY NUTTY/OXIDIZED WINES (Marsala, Madeira, Dry Sherry, Oloroso Sherry, Vermouth, Vin Jaune):** mushroom gravies on chicken and pork chops, rich seafood like halibut and shrimp

3. **SWEET NUTTY/OXIDIZED WINES (Tawny Port, Vin Santo, Cream Sherry, Pedro Ximénez [PX]):** syrups on desserts with nuts, caramel, and vanilla ice cream

4. **SWEET, FORTIFIED RED RUBY PORT:** chocolate sauces, chocolate cakes, Port reduction syrup, and savory Port sauces for steaks with blue cheese

5. **SWEET WHITE WINES (Sauternes, late-harvest whites: Sweet Riesling, Moscato, Ice Wine, Gewürztraminer):** poaching fruit, sweet sauces for fruit tarts, and butter sauces for fish, lobster, and shrimp

6. **MIRIN AND SAKE (Japanese Rice Wine):** marinades, glazes, and Asian barbecue sauce

their wines displayed in a vertical position on the shelf because they assume bottles will not be there long enough for the cork to dry, shrink, and compromise its tight seal. However, if you acquire inventory for at-home storage, it is wise to follow wineries' practice of storing "like" wines together (horizontally on the shelf) arranged in order of their vintage (year they were harvested). This is also called a vertical and makes for quick and easy selection, avoiding unnecessary disturbance to the other quietly aging bottles.

Aging Wine

Aging occurs in multiple phases, and every phase offers a new method to allow aromas, bouquets, and, ultimately, flavors to mature, mingle, and become more complex.

THE FIRST AGING PHASE OCCURS IN THE TANK OR BARREL DURING THE WINEMAKING PROCESS—BEFORE BOTTLING. Some wines are left for a very long time to increase natural layers of flavors. Others may be aged separately, in different oaks, and then blended together just before bottling. Regardless, this first step sets the stage.

THE SECOND PHASE IS CALLED BOTTLE AGING, AND OCCURS AFTER THE WINE HAS BEEN BOTTLED. Complex wines are left undisturbed for much longer periods, where the metamorphosis taking place inside the bottle adds nuances and structure that allow the wine to keep for a very long time. All wines intended for long-term aging will use dark green, thicker glass bottles to filter out light and control environmental factors better. Simpler wines or

BOTTLE OR CASE?

To answer this question, one simply has to determine whether the intention is to drink now or drink later. As with seasonal foods, many wines have limited quantities available. Fans and collectors buy up a supply to have on hand later when the items may no longer be available for purchase.

In addition, sellers often offer discounts for volume purchases, so buying 12 bottles (a case) at the same time means you pay less for each bottle than if you purchased 12 individual bottles over time. A $10 bottle of wine, which totals $120 for a case, would only cost you $96 after a 20 percent case discount. This means you end up paying just $8 a bottle in the end (taxes not included).

If buying wine in bulk, you must also consider proper storage. Savings add up to nothing if your only storage option is a sunny bookshelf beside an air vent near a vibrating massage chair, basically destroying your great investment.

If you have the money, storage space, and enjoy the wine, a case is always the better option.

wines meant to be drunk while still young won't need bottle aging. Wines in clear glass bottles are obvious examples, typically whites, rosés, and light-bodied fruity reds.

THE FINAL AGING OPTION IS THE PURCHASER'S INTENTION. If you begin to collect wine and purposefully store it to maximize the flavor potential of each bottle, sometimes holding on to them for years—or even decades—prior to opening and consuming, then proper consideration needs to occur regarding storage space and conditions.

YOUR PERSONAL WINE "CELLAR"

Personal aging environments should have controlled temperature and humidity, and include minimal light. With these conditions, the wine will slowly enhance structure, develop full flavors, intensify its characteristics, mellow acids and tannins, and improve overall. The more consistent the external environment, the smoother the aging.

Every wine has a target aging window, meaning the amount of time recommended to let it sit and develop before it peaks and should be drunk. All wines tend to plateau about halfway to their peak, when they won't exhibit much change. But the subtle shifts past that stage are noticeable improvements. Once peaked, the wine reverses: flavors and complexity slowly begin to break down, diminishing over time. Many experts enjoy the cat-and-mouse challenge of properly aging wines to precise "sweet spots" for maximum enjoyment.

Graduate

Which Glass for What, and Why?

Not being a wine snob means you don't have to run out and buy 10 styles of glasses in order to accommodate every style of wine. (And, yes, there are even more than 10.) But, at least the next time you're at a wedding or dinner that offers you a choice of shapes, you'll know which one to pick.

Shapes do mean something, and the pros get rather persnickety about which glass goes with what to maximize their olfactory experience. This means the cleanest access to the wine's bouquet and texture without altering temperature or intruding on visual enjoyment.

However, just start with two basics in your home: standard red wine glasses or a white wine shape, which is smaller than those for reds and helps hold in a white's more delicate aroma. If you're a fan of sparkling wines, flutes or tulips are a must.

Fine crystal glassware can be manufactured to be extremely thin and, therefore, allows the most uninhibited access to the wine. But they are a pain to clean, maintain, and store if you have limited space. Many people buy colored glasses made of thick or textured glass. Fine, but those won't allow you to evaluate the color and characteristics of the wine you are drinking.

Every glass has a purpose. The best glasses are clear, stemmed, and feature simple shapes that let the wine breathe according to its style. Roomy bowls are designed to swirl away and work that air-wine combination. Glasses tapered at the top are designed to preserve a bouquet that might otherwise escape. Flutes keep bubbles tight and contained so your sparklings don't go flat.

Stemless tumblers are another popular shape people enjoy for casual gatherings. However, prone to lots of greasy fingerprints, they also warm the wine via your ambient hand heat and interfere with the visuals. That said, they are party-friendly, so if the focus is saving your furniture from "Two Buck Chuck" spills, enjoy away.

Tasting Room Etiquette

Tasting rooms provide access to limited-availability wines, education directly from winemakers, and activities that increase brand loyalty and appreciation. Attendants are not bartenders—they educate buyers and sell wine, period. Fees are charged because a lot of inventory is used for tasting. If your fee gets "comped" (they don't charge you), common courtesy is to buy a bottle—even that $12 picnic pink is an appropriate "Thanks."

TYPES OF GLASSES

BORDEAUX

CABERNET

FLUTE (CHAMPAGNE)

BURGUNDY

PINOT NOIR

STANDARD RED

WHITE BURGUNDY

CHARDONNAY

DESSERT

Wines are poured in a certain order—light to heavy. If a flight (a selection of wines intended for tasting comparison) includes a style you know you won't like, politely ask to substitute another. Pours are typically one ounce—just enough to taste the wine (twice) and determine whether to purchase it. Revisit "Tasting versus Drinking" (see page 27), but, in place of swallowing, gently spit the wine into the vessel provided. Though awkward at first, spitting indicates you are serious and want to avoid inebriation and resulting bad purchases.

If celebrating a social occasion, you will not be judged for swallowing what's in your glass. But beware of PALATE FATIGUE—a condition occurring when too much alcohol and too many mixed flavors prevent one from adequately tasting anything.

Tips of any amount are optional but always appreciated when allowed.

Restaurant Etiquette

Keep these basic guidelines in mind when ordering wine in a dining or drinking establishment:

The host, person who ordered, or purchaser tastes first. Additional tasters are optional. While pros are concerned with myriad technical terms and ritual formalities, you need only focus on three activities: look, smell (the wine, not the cork), and taste.

LOOK

The server, or SOMM (short for *sommelier*, pronounced roughly sum-all-YAY), a trained wine specialist, separate from your food server, "presents" the bottle. The taster verifies it is the same as requested, and that the label information matches: confirm name, type of wine, and year. A simple nod or "yes" keeps things moving.

Next, the bottle is opened in your presence. While every detail has a role, this just assures you no substitutions occurred. (Bonus points if the cork removal is silent—"popping" is bad form.)

Do not smell the cork when it is presented. Corks provide seasoned pros with visual evidence (black streaks, crumbly edges, etc.) of storage snafus, alerting them to pay attention when tasting. To you, however, it is a mere souvenir.

SMELL AND TASTE

Swirl, smell, and taste to confirm the wine is not flawed before the server pours it for the remaining guests. You are "quality assurance."

Why Pairings Matter

There are no hard and fast rules, but general guidelines exist for appreciating wine and food together so you experience compatibility without forcing your senses to keep up.

All worlds of food and wine are mixing and merging these days, so old codes such as "match the wine's color to the meat" (i.e., white wine with fish, chicken, and pork; red wine with beef and game) are out. The goal is to land on enough pleasing outcomes that you look forward to consuming certain combinations because they enhance each other.

WINE-FOOD PAIRING

WINE	PAIRING
German Rieslings	Indian curries and spicy Asian food Leafy, sweet greens and stems Most versatile for pairing with North American spicy foods—from chicken mole to shrimp fajitas Raw root veggies
Full, unoaked Chardonnays	Charbroiled meats Cooked root vegetables Greens (fresh or cooked)
Acidic, sometimes sweet whites: Chablis, Pinot Grigio, Sauvignon Blanc, Viognier	Acidic foods using citrus flavors like lemon, lime, grapefruit Chèvre Clams, catfish, sole Dishes with spicy chilies or Indian, Thai, and Vietnamese spices Squash and peppers Sushi
Oaked Chardonnays	Cheeses like Brie, Camembert, Cheddars, Gruyère, Monterey Jack
Champagnes	Brie Camembert Caviar Desserts Lobster Truffles (fungus or chocolate varieties—likely not together)
Rosés	Fruit Hot-weather snacking Picnic foods Salsas Spicy dishes
Merlots	Barbecued and grilled fish Simply prepared fowl and red meats

WINE	PAIRING
Pinot Noirs	Anything "smoked" or barbecued Mushrooms, "earthy" flavors, mustards Pork and game meats Some fish: mahimahi, salmon, swordfish
Cabernet Sauvignons	Stronger, older cheeses Strongly flavored meat-based dishes
Italian Reds	Acidic entrées featuring tomatoes: many red pasta dishes, pizzas, salty, or fatty dishes Gorgonzola and Parmesan cheeses Rabbit
Spanish Wines	Salty or cured foods like olives, firm cheeses (Mahon, Iberico, Manchego), and pork hams and sausages
Ruby Ports	Dried fruit, milk chocolate, walnuts
Tawny Ports	Darker chocolate, bananas, cream, caramel, nutmeg, and cinnamon Pecorino Romano cheese
Vintage Ports	Walnuts, Roquefort and Stilton cheeses (or enjoy alone)

Start by matching the entrée and wine weights. A slab of lasagna outweighs a plain, grilled chicken breast any day. As a rough guide, lighter wine styles tend to be at the start of a wine menu's sections and work their way toward richer, fuller-bodied wines—which also tend to be higher in alcohol (13-plus percent).

Next, consider flavor intensity. Flavorful wines will dominate a subtle dish—and vice versa, making one less desirable than the other. Match big or subtle wine flavors using the entrée as the guide.

Remember, there are no mistakes: live (and drink!) and learn.

What to Do with Leftover Wine

You have leftover wine. (This is possible?) Now what?

DRINK, COOK, CLEAN, OR CREATE

OPTION ONE, CONTINUE DRINKING LATER. Flip the same cork you removed from the bottle and put it back in the bottle until snug. Drink within 24 hours. A step up in preserving the wine is spraying inert gas into the bottle before recorking. (Private Preserve is the brand used most in wineries.) This barrier of harmless gas prevents oxygen from affecting the wine until you drink it again. However, it is still recommended to drink within two days. Avoid vacuum pumps; they suck out aromas, and are not preferred by experts.

OPTION TWO, SAVE FOR COOKING. Not drinking within a couple of days? Cork it and refrigerate it for use (within a couple of weeks) in your next culinary experiment. A chef's staple, cooking with wine kicks flavor up a notch. Add to sauces and soups. Reduce by boiling and simmering to a thicker consistency for excellent glazes and drizzles. Poach fruits or vegetables in it. Shake vigorously with oil and vinegar to give zip to a salad dressing. Freeze in ice cube trays and pop out a cube when you need it, up to three months later. There are plenty of online recipes and resources with delicious, edible ideas.

OPTION THREE, CLEAN. Clean grills: Tough grease spots dissolve with leftover white wine plus baking soda—a great degreasing solution. Clean yourself, too: Add up to two cups of red wine to the bathtub before you soak for healthy antioxidants and beneficial skin nutrients.

WHAT ARE WINE CLUBS?

Wine clubs began as vehicles to showcase portfolio wines not widely available in wineries or through retailers, or to introduce brands and styles to consumers who, hopefully, would enjoy them and purchase more of that brand.

Nowadays, it seems everyone offers a wine club—even airlines. While motives are pretty clear-cut (generate revenue), clubs are worth checking out, if you know what you want to get out of one. By joining, you agree to purchase and receive regular shipments of wine. The club stores your information and charges your credit card for the cost of each shipment, (wine plus shipping costs), just prior to sending the bottles. Tiers and options allow you to pre-set style preferences and budgets for your shipments. Extra member perks are based on commitment levels: discounts, merchandise, no-fee tastings, VIP events, promotions, etc.

A winery club only sends wines from that winery or its sister brands, providing access to hard-to-obtain varietals and library wines (reserve wines from older vintages).

Retail clubs send wines from across a large number of properties and labels, based on that club's theme.

OPTION FOUR, CREATE. Release your inner artist using wine as an artistic medium. Wine can be used as a stainer on poured concrete, wood, fabric, painters' canvases, paper, and in papermaking, with amazing results. (Make sure to wash surfaces thoroughly once desired color is achieved, or you'll attract lots of new four- and six-legged visitors.) Correct nasty stains on shirts and throw pillows by soaking the item in full-strength or diluted wine until a uniform color is achieved. (Launder afterward.)

Hangovers (and Their Cures)

Okay, that slew of new wines yesterday is haunting you this morning. Everyone swears by "secret cures," but remedies need to address several factors.

Alcohol triggers immune system responses causing inflammation, and CONGENERS (fermentation byproducts found in red wine and brown liquors) also cause inflammation. Anti-inflammatory painkillers tackle this (ibuprofen or aspirin).

Dehydration. The fact remains: Alcohol dehydrates cells; water does not. Besides flushing your system, water also transports oxygen to gasping cells, counteracting the lowered blood pressure resulting from dilated blood vessels.

Alcohol increases stomach acid production while slowing the stomach down. "Coat" it before drinking by eating foods naturally containing fat and protein, instead of carbohydrates. After drinking, eat bland foods to help neutralize acids.

Falling blood-sugar levels cause shakiness, moodiness, and fatigue. Exercise also depletes blood sugar and actually worsens symptoms. Ingest quick, small doses of "sweet" every couple of hours: fruit, a handful of raisins, a half cup of juice (no diet soda), one tablespoon of sugar or honey, hard candy or jellybeans, etc.

A hangover has to run its course. Rest, water, anti-inflammatory painkillers, and simply waiting it out are the most consistent cures (therapeutic benefits of a breakfast burrito notwithstanding).

BUILD A DATABASE OF
WINES CONSUMED

Everyone is guilty of forgetting the name of that to-die-for wine their host pulled out at last night's dinner party. It helps to write down or photograph wines you've consumed—whether to look for it again or recall whether you enjoyed something you are certain you've purchased before. Record the winery, type of grape, country, and vintage. Create a rudimentary "Ranking" or "Notes" section to which you can refer as well. Motivated? Add a space to include where you purchased it and what you paid.

Depending on the level of sophistication you fancy, this can be as simple as a clipboard with some paper and a pen, a dedicated notebook or journal, an online file for images and notes, or an actual app purchased for one of your devices. If you *really* get into it, there are sophisticated home-cellar management software programs such as cellartracker.com, which adds access to fellow wine drinkers who enjoy "geeking out" on wine experiences with other wine enthusiasts.

INDEX